*For Dad,*
*and your monumental support.*

BIG PICTURE PRESS

First published in the UK in 2018 by Big Picture Press,
This flexiback edition printed in 2021
by Big Picture Press,
an imprint of Bonnier Books UK,
The Plaza, 535 King's Road, London, SW10 0SZ
Owned by Bonnier Books
Sveavägen 56, Stockholm, Sweden
www.templarco.co.uk/big-picture-press
www.bonnierbooks.co.uk

ISBN 978-1-78741-776-2 (Flexiback)
ISBN 978-1-78741-052-7 (Hardback)
ISBN 978-1-78741-378-8 (eBook)

This book was typeset in BlockyJames Infant
The illustrations were created and coloured digitally

Designed by Helen Chapman
Edited by Joanna McInerney

Consultant: Rupert Matthews

Printed in China

MIX
Paper from
responsible sources
FSC® C104723

# Meet the ...

# ANCIENT ROMANS

BPP

# CONTENTS

The Roman Empire began in, well, Rome! It was one of the greatest the world had ever seen. For nearly 500 years, a huge chunk of Europe was ruled by the emperors of Rome, who led mighty armies in their quest for even more power.

The Romans gave us canals and straight roads, but they also gave us gladiators, baths and shopping centres. What made Rome so great? What did gladiators do? Why did everyone wear sandals? Let's explore from the beginning.

FELINE FRIENDS

CAESAR

The Romans had a myth, or story, about how their city began. Gather round everyone.

1. Romulus and Remus (sons of the god Mars) were babies when their evil uncle left them to drown in the river Tiber.

2. Thankfully, a she-wolf rescued them and protected them while they grew up.

3. When they were older, Romulus and Remus took revenge on their horrid uncle and killed him.

4. When that was done, they decided to start a new city, but couldn't agree on where to put it.

5. The brothers looked for a sign from the gods to see which of them had the best plan, but that didn't work either.

6. They argued constantly, and one day got into a fight after Remus made fun of Romulus.

7. Remus was killed in the fight, so Romulus got his way and built the new city overlooking the Tiber. He then modestly named the new place after himself. Way to go, Romulus . . . bad luck, Remus!

At first Rome was ruled by kings, but it later became a republic, which meant no one person was in charge. Instead, a group of rich men called senators ran the empire and made all the decisions.

The senators were greedy and wanted more power and money. Tired of answering to other states, they started fights that lasted hundreds of years. Not good news for the people of Rome.

Rome's greatest rival was Carthage in North Africa. The battles between them lasted for almost 20 years. In 218 BC, the fearsome general Hannibal led a huge army and 37 elephants to attack. But Rome was too tough and Carthage was defeated and burned.

Rome went on to defeat other powerful states, growing bigger, richer and stronger. But as they won more battles, the senators started to fight amongst themselves . . . it would be their downfall in the end.

The only way to bring peace back to Rome was to end the republic and put one person back in charge. This person was called an emperor. He ruled over everything, controlling the government, armies and religion. Emperors ruled Rome for the next 500 years.

That looks nothing like me!

With no Internet or TV to show the public what the emperor looked like, statues and coins were produced with his image instead. Hopefully they were flattering, as they couldn't be changed later!

MR NERO

Some emperors were loved by the public, but others were considered monsters, or just a bit weird. The good, the bad, and the mad – here are some of Rome's most famous emperors:

### AUGUSTUS
#### 27 BC – AD 14

Augustus was the first emperor of Rome. He wasn't very loveable, but he rebuilt Rome after all the fighting, established an army and brought peace back to the land. What a guy!

### CALIGULA
#### AD 37 – 41

Caligula was a violent leader who went mad with wealth and power. He once tried to put his horse in charge of the government! He was killed by his own bodyguards who decided to put a stop to him.

### CLAUDIUS
#### AD 41 – 54

Claudius was disabled and had trouble walking and speaking. At first he wasn't taken very seriously, but he turned out to be a great leader, expanding the empire and conquering Britain.

You may be wondering why Julius Caesar isn't here amongst these other famous emperors. Well, that's because although Caesar was a powerful man, he was never actually an emperor. We'll find out more about him on pages 16 and 17.

## HADRIAN
### AD 76 - 138

Hadrian was a clever general. He made the empire easier to defend and built a giant wall between England and Scotland to try and keep the people of the north out. Parts of the wall still stand today!

## NERO
### AD 54 - 68

Nero wanted to be a celebrity, but when he appeared on stage many people thought it was a bit silly. He didn't seem to care when a huge fire destroyed the city in AD 64, and the people turned on him.

## TRAJAN
### AD 98 - 117

Trajan was Spanish, and one of the most successful emperors. Rome was at its largest and most wealthy when he reigned. He was declared 'the best ruler' by the Roman council. Cool!

Julius Caesar is one of the most famous names from Roman history. William Shakespeare even wrote a play about him! Caesar was a brilliant military general who wanted to be an emperor, but was killed before it could happen. These are some of the reasons why we remember him:

1. He was the first person to have his portrait put onto a coin. What a trendsetter!

2. The calendar we use today was invented by Caesar, and the month of July is named after him (*Julius* - get it?).

3. Caesar was a bit of a show-off, and had quite a few enemies. He fought with another Roman leader called Pompey for nearly two years. In Egypt, a young pharaoh called Ptolemy VIII had Pompey killed and presented his head to Caesar as a gift.

4. While in Egypt, Caesar fell in love with the queen, Cleopatra. He helped her become a pharaoh and had a child with her.

5. In 75 BC, Caesar was captured by pirates! He was kept prisoner until his friends could pay the money that the pirates demanded. Once he was freed, Caesar returned with an army and put the pirates in jail, before having them killed.

6. Caesar listened to the people of Rome and didn't agree with the rules that the senators made. During his reign as leader, he gave land and jobs to the poorer citizens of Rome.

7. He was declared leader of Rome for the rest of his life in 45 BC. But unfortunately, the next year he was killed by a group who thought he had grown too powerful. What terrible luck!

The Roman army, led by the emperor, was one of the most successful in history. The main division was called the legion. It was made up of about 5,500 skilled soldiers called legionaries.

Oh good grief, what am I called again?

The legions were divided into smaller groups of 80 men called centuries. The leader of each century was called a centurion.

Wait for me!

Are we there yet? We've been marching for DAYS!

## Roman Soldier Tool Kit:

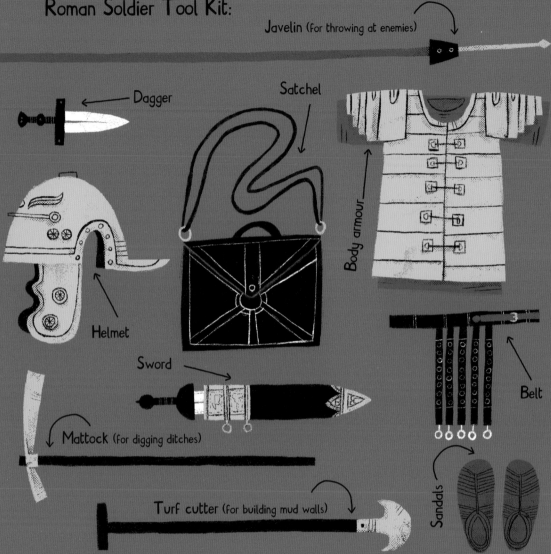

Javelin (for throwing at enemies)

Dagger

Satchel

Body armour

Helmet

Sword

Belt

Mattock (for digging ditches)

Turf cutter (for building mud walls)

Sandals

Legionaries had to be brave warriors and extremely fit. In addition to heavy iron armour, they would carry equipment weighing 40kg on their backs, and would sometimes walk 30km in a day. That's like walking across London, England carrying an adult baboon!

Roman soldiers were lean, mean, fighting machines. They could march all day, swim across rivers, then smash into enemy forts, all before dinner. After that, they would build a camp surrounded by holes and wooden spikes, and in the morning they'd do it all again!

You had to do what you were told in the Roman army. Anyone found messing around or sleeping on duty would face tough punishments, or even death. However, it was often a much better life than working on a farm for little pay.

Family was very important to the Romans. Men were in charge and took control of everything their family did. Women ran the home, paid the bills, cooked meals and looked after the children. Phew!

It was common for pets to be found scurrying around too. Cats and dogs were kept as companions for children but they also chased away the rats that would steal food.

Larger, richer families might have had slaves to do the work. Many slaves had hard lives, but some were treated well — like one of the family. Today, we think the idea of slavery is terrible, but Ancient Rome relied on it. From washing up to building temples, the Romans might not have got much done without slaves.

Oops . . .

Most Roman families lived in crowded apartment blocks made of cheap wood and mud bricks. There was no running water and up to seven people would share a bedroom. What if someone snored? Fire was a constant risk, so cooking had to be done outside.

Wealthy Romans had it much better. They lived in villas away from crowded cities, where servants did all the work. They had running water, heating and even flushing toilets! Unfortunately though, toilet paper hadn't been invented yet, so rich Romans had to use a sponge on a stick. Not so glamorous!

Ancient Roman clothing was pretty different to yours or mine. They didn't wear trainers or jeans. Instead, men and women wore loose woollen garments called tunics and leather sandals because it was hot nearly all the time.

This looks great on you!

To look extra smart, men could wear a toga. This was a really long piece of cloth which was wrapped around the body. Togas were extremely heavy and uncomfortable. If only they had invented the shirt!

Most of the clothes in Rome were made from wool, which could be made quite easily at home. Woolly underpants included!

Women wore lots of jewellery to show off their wealth. It was also fashionable to look very pale, so they covered their faces with chalk or poisonous white lead! For eyeliner, some women used ash made from burnt wood, followed by some red powdered clay for their cheeks. Worst make-up ever!

Only rich families sent their children to school and most girls stayed at home. If boys wanted to study, they had to go to school seven days a week. No thanks! Northern Europeans hadn't written anything down before the Romans came and introduced the Latin alphabet — they had to remember everything instead — so writing was very important at school too.

villa

feles

canis

arbor

The Romans wrote on all sorts of surfaces including wood, papyrus and stone. Paper didn't exist yet! Books were rare and expensive because each one had to be written by hand.

The Romans didn't use numbers like we do. Instead, they used capital letters to count and do sums. Unfortunately for us, this has made things quite confusing!

They used these letters:

| I | V | X | L | C | D | M |
|---|---|---|---|---|---|---|
| 1 | 5 | 10 | 50 | 100 | 500 | 1000 |

and combined them to form more numbers, like this:

I = 1          II = 2          III = 3          IV = 4          V = 5
VI = 6          VII = 7          VIII = 8          IX = 9          X = 10

Confused yet? Well, the rules are that a letter **AFTER** a larger letter means you add it. A letter **BEFORE** a larger one means you take it away.

So XI is 10 + 1 = 11 and IX is 10 – 1 = 9

Phew, what a headache! After all that, let's get something to eat . . .

  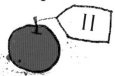

Oh, never mind.

Farming was an important part of Roman culture and men, women and children would work endlessly gathering crops in the intense heat. They also grew olives and grapes for making wine, kept cows and goats for milk and cheese, and kept bees for honey.

The Romans didn't eat sitting at a table, but instead lazed on beds and ate with their fingers. Luxury! Some foods sound similar to things we'd eat today (like sausages), but others sound much less appealing. Cow brains or dormouse covered in honey, anyone?

Crops were valuable as they could also be traded with other countries. Food and spices were sent across the empire and beyond. In return, Romans would receive materials they couldn't make themselves, like silk from China and papyrus from Egypt.

Get your grapes! Best grapes in the world!

I love grapes! Trade you for this lovely silk?

The Romans were very clever and made some big developments in science and technology, Some of the things they invented still make our lives easier today.

## CONCRETE

This sounds boring, but at the time concrete was a big deal and very useful. With concrete, the Romans could expand their empire by building roads, bridges and aqueducts (which we'll find out more about on page 47) — many of which we still use.

## HEATING

This was supplied by slaves. They kept a constant fire going beneath the floorboards, so that the heat would spread through spaces under floors and between walls, keeping those rich people upstairs nice and warm.

## CALENDAR

The calendar as we know it today was invented by Julius Caesar. Before he came along, the calendar was a mess, with priests removing and adding months wherever they liked. It was a crazy system and no one ever knew when their birthday was. Imagine that! Caesar fixed this by taking the Egyptian calendar and making it his. His calendar had 365 days just like ours.

## BALLISTAS

These powerful giant crossbows were originally a Greek invention, but the Romans took the idea and made it even deadlier. The largest ballista could fire stones or bolts up to 1,000 metres, crushing enemy armies and buildings alike. Run for cover!

Because the Romans fought so much, the army developed some of the earliest known hospitals, where nurses were trained to treat wounds. Doctors could fix broken bones, amputate limbs and remove lumps and bumps. But, with no anaesthetics to put you to sleep, surgery would be nearly impossible and terrifying to go through!

Despite knowing more about the human body, the Romans still didn't understand what caused illnesses and blamed curses, angry gods or witchcraft. If you were ill, you were given some herbal medicine or told to have a healing bath.

Due to bad diets and poor living conditions, the people of Ancient Rome didn't usually live for very long — if they lived past ten they were lucky, if they lived to 35 they were doing really well. The average life expectancy today is 71! How things change.

At first, the Romans didn't really get the idea of only worshipping one god — they worshipped hundreds! If they wanted something, they would offer sacrifices to one of them, whether it was courage for a battle, a bit more money or some nice new shoes.

If someone stole your dinner money or gave you a bad haircut, you could write a message to the gods about how annoying they were on a curse tablet. These were sheets of lead or other metals, which were rolled up and thrown into sacred pools in temples. Hopefully the gods would read them and punish your enemy.

This is for saying I smell bad!

Well this is for smelling really bad!

Later, Romans began to follow the religion Christianity, which we will find out more about on pages 40 and 41.

Romans originally worshipped hundreds of gods and goddesses, including some from Greece and Egypt. Each one controlled a different part of daily life. Some of the most important gods were:

**NEPTUNE**
God of the sea

**JUPITER**
God of the sky

**JUNO**
Goddess of women

**VENUS**
Goddess of beauty

Have you noticed that some gods have the same names as planets? Well, all of the planets except for Earth were actually named after Roman gods. Jupiter, Saturn, Mars, Venus and Mercury were given their names thousands of years ago. The Romans could see these planets without a telescope and you can still see them today!

DIANA
Goddess of hunting

MERCURY
God of travellers and thieves

MARS
God of war

BACCHUS
God of wine and partying

Worshipping anything other than the gods was against the law for a long time in Ancient Rome. Despite this, Christianity quickly became popular. Christians promised that if you lived a good life you would go to heaven. In the other Roman religion, only the gods could live in heaven and normal people would go to the underworld, which didn't sound as nice.

In AD 313, Emperor Constantine I had a dream. It was the night before a battle and he was super stressed out. How was he going to beat an army twice the size of his?

When he eventually got to sleep, a voice in his dream told him that he'd win if he fought under the sign of the Christian religion.

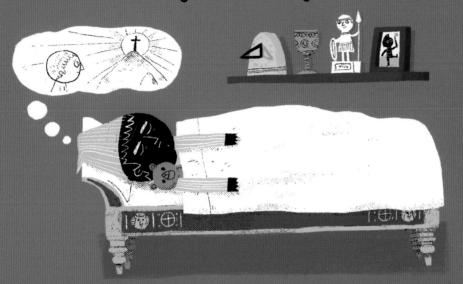

In the morning, he made his soldiers paint Christian symbols on their shields and they quickly and easily won the battle! Hurrah! Constantine took control of Rome and went on to make Christianity the official religion.

A lot of what we know about the people of Ancient Rome
is taken from paintings, sculptures and mosaics.

Wealthy Romans also displayed
busts around their home to show
off the portraits of their ancestors.
A bust is a sculpture of just the
head and shoulders of a person.

I'm watching you . . .

Emperors would often have
sculptures made of themselves
and placed around the city.
They did this to remind the
people who was in charge.

Mosaics were pictures made from
small coloured tiles. Sometimes
thousands of tiles would be used
to make a picture, or a pattern.
It seems the Romans had a lot
of time on their hands!

Music was played at religious ceremonies, parties and gladiator shows. It's impossible to know what Roman music sounded like, because they didn't make any albums, but it's fun to imagine what it might have sounded like. Instruments include pan pipes, flutes, trumpets and cymbals. What a racket!

Going to the theatre was another popular pastime in Rome. Most plays were comedies, but there were serious tragedies too. Tickets were free, but were very hard to get hold of.

Plays often went on for hours, so the actors jumped about and shouted to keep the audience interested. They often held up happy or sad masks to help the audience understand what was going on.

The Romans were master builders who made structures from stone, brick, marble and concrete. They even invented the dome. The skill and detail that went into the buildings they created is still impressive today. Marble-ous!

Romans were also brilliant engineers, constructing roads and bridges, and building aqueducts to carry water to cities.

Aqueducts look like a huge bridge made of many arches. The channel on top allows water to flow along, where it ends up as drinking water, toilet water or food for plants. Very clever.

Hey, it works!

STEAM ROOM

Hey! That's my best toga!

Roman houses didn't have baths or showers. Instead, every city had a public bath where people came to get clean. Imagine bathing with loads of other people — awkward! Men and women bathed at separate times however, so it was slightly less embarrassing.

COLD BATHS

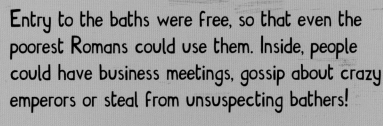

Entry to the baths were free, so that even the poorest Romans could use them. Inside, people could have business meetings, gossip about crazy emperors or steal from unsuspecting bathers!

Soap hadn't been invented yet so people used olive oil to clean themselves, which they'd then scrape off with a stick. Lovely.

The Romans loved chariot racing. Chariots were small two-wheeled carts, driven by one man and pulled by two or four horses. In the early days of Rome, chariot races were held on the streets, but this was too dangerous for the racers and the public, so the Romans built racecourses instead.

I can't giddy up!

The biggest and best racecourse was the Circus Maximus in Rome, Italy. Watched by 250,000 people, the chariots galloped and crashed their way through seven gruelling laps. Only the best charioteers made it to the Circus Maximus and it was considered a great honour to race there.

Another spectator sport in Rome was the gladiator fights. These were so popular that grand arenas had to be built for the huge crowds to fit into. The largest and most famous amphitheatre is the enormous Colosseum in Rome, Italy, which opened in AD 80.

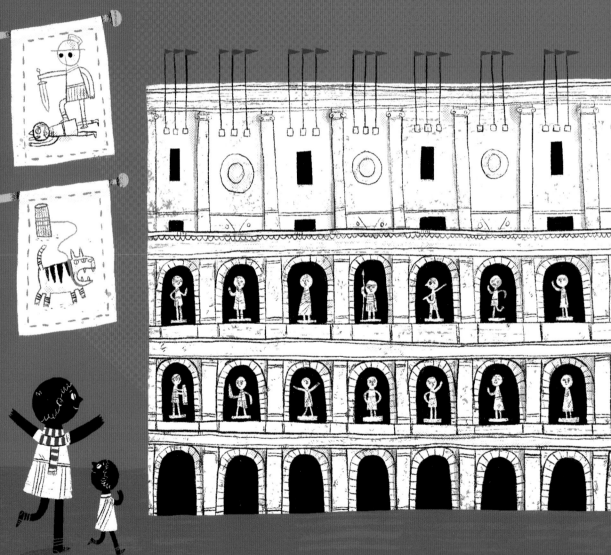

It could hold 50,000 spectators, who didn't have to pay an entrance fee. The events — and sometimes the food — were paid for by the emperor or other important Romans to try and earn the respect of the people. Nice!

Gladiator games were a huge attraction. Inside the great arenas, gladiators would fight to the death while the crowds cheered on - the audience actually thought this was fun! Slaves were sent to a gladiator boot camp, where they trained until they were ready.

Sorry buddy . . .
Emperor's orders.

Training was tough and the punishment for failing was worse,
so why on Earth did they volunteer? Well, some slaves wanted
to win prizes, get rich, or earn enough money to buy their freedom
– if only they'd invented Roman's Got Talent instead!

A day at the arena began with a huge parade and some light-hearted warm-up acts, including jugglers, acrobats and even performing monkeys and elephants. Then things got more serious as animals fought other animals or trained animal fighters.

In the afternoon, the gladiators fought. There were different types of gladiator; some were heavily armoured with shields and helmets, others didn't have much protection but carried long tridents instead.

Secutor

Retiarius

Provocator

Murmillo

Crupellarius

When a gladiator had beaten his opponent, he would stop the fight and raise his hand. The emperor asked the audience what he should do — spare the fallen gladiator or have him killed. A smart emperor would agree with the audience — if he didn't there could be a riot.

The Roman Empire lasted for about 1,000 years. The bigger it got, the harder it became for rulers to keep control over everything. Emperors were becoming more selfish and lazy, and the army was tired. Constant battles took their toll on the Roman forces and everything started to crumble.

Yawn. Now that the Empire's over, can I get some sleep?

The last emperor was Romulus Augustus, who lost his power in AD 476 to a German prince called Flavius Odoacer. He was mocked by the public and nicknamed 'Little Emperor'. The Germans took over and the empire was split up amongst other kings and princes from outside Italy. This was the end of the Empire.

Today, Rome is a busy modern city and one of the most visited places in the world. Thousands of years later, there are still signs of the ancient past. Temples, villas and columns can be found around every corner and you can still see the ruins of the Colosseum. What's more, it's the best place in the world to get an ice cream!

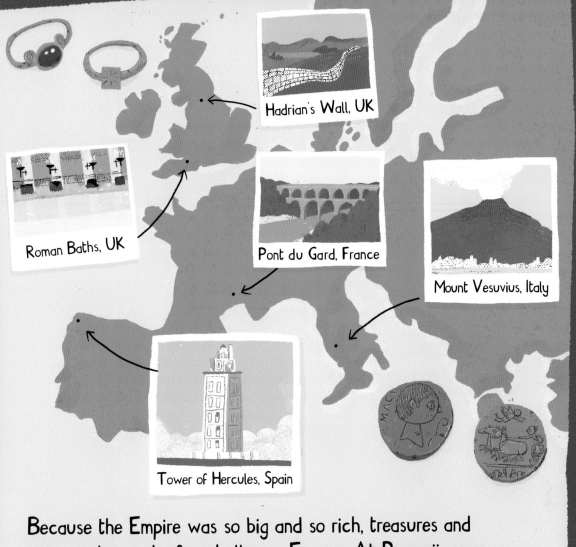

Hadrian's Wall, UK

Roman Baths, UK

Pont du Gard, France

Mount Vesuvius, Italy

Tower of Hercules, Spain

Because the Empire was so big and so rich, treasures and monuments can be found all over Europe. At Pompeii, near Vesuvius, Italy, you can walk around a Roman city preserved by ash. In Bath, England, you can visit the Roman baths, one of the finest remains still standing today. There are also artefacts in museums all around the world, giving us a glimpse of this powerful and important civilisation.

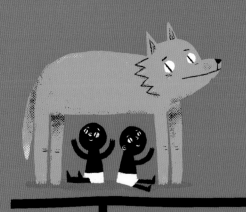

**753 BC**
According to legend, twin brothers Romulus and Remus found Rome.

**509 BC**
Rome becomes a republic, governed by a group of senators.

**264–146 BC**
Rome and Carthage fight for years in the bloody Punic Wars.

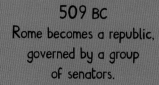

**27 BC**
Augustus becomes Rome's first emperor.

**AD 43–84**
Rome invades and conquers Britain.

**AD 79**
The Colosseum is opened in Rome.

**51 BC**
General Julius Caesar
conquers Gaul
(modern-day France).

**45 BC**
Caesar becomes ruler
of Rome. He dies
a year later.

**AD 306**
Constantine I
becomes Rome's first
Christian emperor.

**AD 476**
Armies from Germany
invade Rome. It's the end
of the Roman Empire.

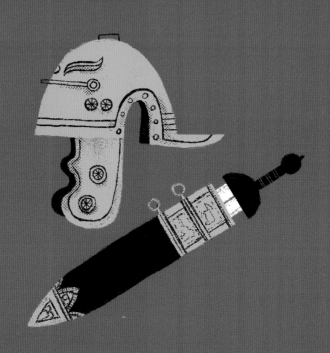

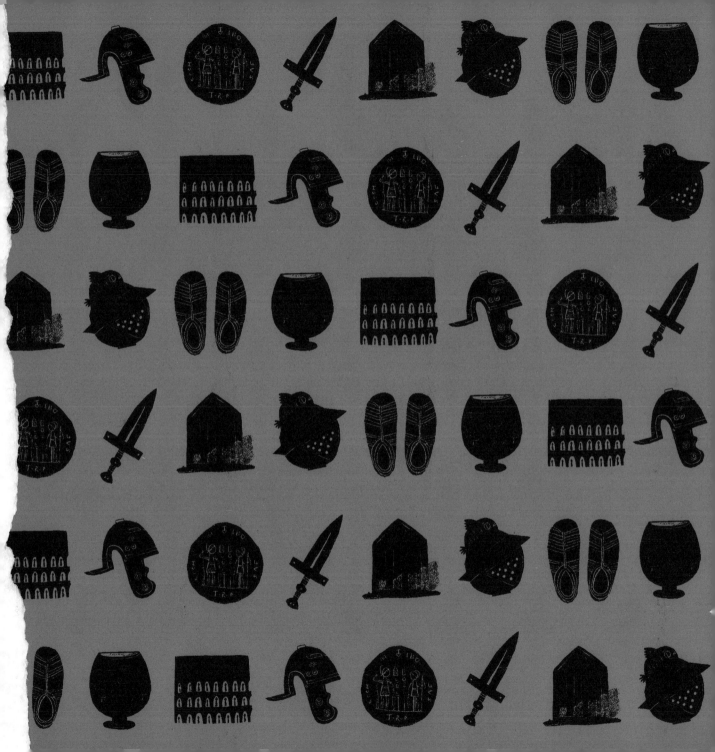

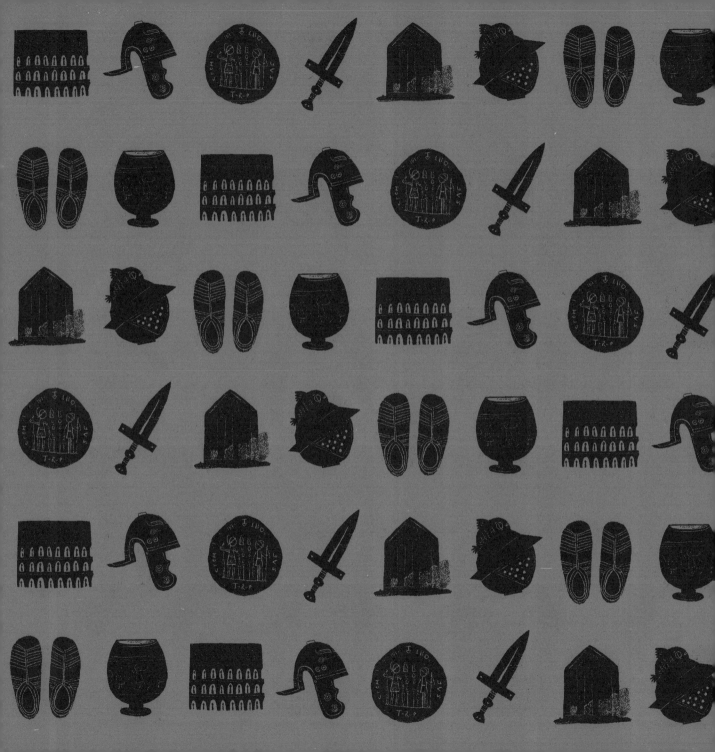